BELIEVE IN THE BEAUTY OF YOUR DREAMS

A DIARY TO UPLIFT SELF

SNEHA BANDARU

BALBOA.PRESS

A DIVISION OF HAY HOUSE

Balboa Press books may be ordered through booksellers or by contacting:

Balboa Press
A Division of Hay House
1663 Liberty Drive
Bloomington, IN 47403
www.balboapress.com
844-682-1282

Because of the dynamic nature of the Internet, any web addresses or
links contained in this book may have changed since publication and
may no longer be valid. The views expressed in this work are solely those
of the author and do not necessarily reflect the views of the publisher,
and the publisher hereby disclaims any responsibility for them.

The author of this book does not dispense medical advice or prescribe the use
of any technique as a form of treatment for physical, emotional, or medical
problems without the advice of a physician, either directly or indirectly. The
intent of the author is only to offer information of a general nature to help
you in your quest for emotional and spiritual well-being. In the event you use
any of the information in this book for yourself, which is your constitutional
right, the author and the publisher assume no responsibility for your actions.

Any people depicted in stock imagery provided by Getty Images are
models, and such images are being used for illustrative purposes only.
Certain stock imagery © Getty Images.

Print information available on the last page.

ISBN: 979-8-7652-5392-2 (sc)
ISBN: 979-8-7652-5393-9 (hc)
ISBN: 979-8-7652-5394-6 (e)

Library of Congress Control Number: 2024914885

Balboa Press rev. date: 07/26/2024

> *Today is going to be awesome*
> **99**

Embrace your authentic self. Your greatest power comes from being who you truly are.

Don't believe in limitations or fear. Believe in yourself and in faith.

♥ *Just for today, in everything you do, in everything you say, be the blessing the world needs today.*

The power of decision is the first step to manifesting the life you desire. The universe has your back.

Leave the past behind, don't get lost in future thoughts, anchor your mind in the present.

Life is happening NOW, this moment.

The present moment is the moment. Do your best. Be your best. You are here today because of your past moment actions. You will be where you want to be because of your present moment, actions, and thoughts. Use this moment wisely.

Life is a game, not a war. In a war, victory decides your happiness in the end. Unlike war, approaching life as a game means embracing uncertainty, celebrating small victories, and learning from setbacks. It's an invitation to play with passion, curiosity, and a sense of adventure. Roll the dice, navigate the board, and savor the journey, for in the end, it's not about winning or losing; it's about how well we played the game.

In a world where diversity thrives, every form of ability has its own unique strength.

One can achieve seemingly impossible tasks when they believe in themselves. This confidence dawns when someone anchors their faith in something unchanging—the self. The self is the soul, a piece of God; thus, faith in oneself is, in essence, faith in God.

♥ Never Give up because great things take time.

Wear a 'never say die' attitude in the face of challenges.

Mind is the limit.

Life's equation: 10% events, 90% your chosen responses to the events.

Thoughts are more painful than deeds.

♥♥ *Live for today. Plan for tomorrow. Party to Night.*

Hobbies become habits, habits become character, character becomes destiny.

Be patient, everything comes to you at the right moment.

♥ *Love does not need to be perfect. It just needs to be true.*

Give miracles a chance in your life.

There is no life without ups and downs.

Habits of Highly Successful Individuals:

* *Daily Goal Setting*

* *Be Results Oriented*

* *Be People Oriented*

* *Stay Health Oriented*

* *Work with Integrity*

* *Self-Disciplined*

* *Consistent with the routine*

The skill of motivating yourself to do what needs to be done, when it needs to be done, regardless of how you feel about it is productivity mindset.

Life Habits for Prosperity and Personal Development:

* *Positive Self-Concept: Rich people cultivate a positive self-image.*

* *Comfort Zone Expansion: They regularly venture beyond their comfort zones.*

* *Positive Thinking: Sustaining a positive mindset is a constant practice.*

* *High Self-Ideal: They strive for a lofty self-ideal, setting ambitious standards for themselves.*

There's a truth behind 'Just Kidding,' a touch of emotion behind 'I don't care,' a hint of pain behind 'It's Okay,' a hidden 'I NEED YOU' behind 'Leave me Alone,' and a multitude of unspoken words behind 'The Silence'.

At times, you simply need to be done—neither mad nor upset. Just move on.

In a relationship, your extra efforts will not compensate for their lack of effort.

You can tell you have made the right choice when your body feels lighter, and your mind is at peace.

I may not be perfect, I may say and do goofy things, and my funny bone makes me laugh at the wrong times. My heart bears scars from those who caused me pain. I'm a little quirky and likely won't change. Love me or not, one thing is for sure: If I love you, I'll do it with all my heart ♥.

You are born alone. You will die alone. You have to walk your path alone.

Whether you become a victim of your life narrative or a victor, it's entirely your choice. You are responsible for your life.

Don't let feelings decide your state of mind. Train your mind to be untouched and unattached.

When someone speaks, you know what's on their mind. When someone does something for you, you know what's in their heart. If words and actions don't align, they don't have good intentions for you.

Karma has no menu. It serves only what you deserve.

Karma: Cultivate positive thoughts, speak kind words, and do good for others. The universe reciprocates.

A strong person does not seek revenge. They move on and let the karma do the dirty work.

Karma has a boomerang effect. It shows up when least expected. Keep doing the good you are doing, for what goes around comes around.

Power of Positive Thinking:

The Universe does not respond to language; it responds to vibrational frequency. Your subconscious mind does not distinguish between 'I' and 'they,' so what you think, you attract. For goodness' sake, avoid thoughts of jealousy, greed, and lack. Always focus on blessings, abundance, happiness, forgiveness, and healing for <u>yourself and others</u>*. What you think, you attract. Each of the above vices has its own low vibration, keeping you in the same vibration.*

This too shall pass...

After every SAD day comes a GLAD day.
Keep smiling.

Weak individuals seek revenge, strong individuals forgive, and the intelligent ones choose to ignore and move on with life.

A disciplined mind fosters focus, cultivates resilience, paves the way for a content life, and brings happiness.

If you cannot change a situation, change your perspective, and adjust your attitude.

Anger for others is a self-imposed punishment for oneself.

People in pain often inflict pain on others. Disrupt the cycle of misery and distress by embracing compassion and forgiveness.

And when I'm finally tired of trying, I'll just leave. No fights, no arguments, and sometimes not even a goodbye.

♥♥ *When you fully trust someone, you finally get a lifelong connection or a lasting lesson.*

....

....

Even loss and betrayal can bring about awakening and elevate us to the next level of growth.

....

....

Sometimes the hardest thing and the right thing are the same.

....

....

Never underestimate the potential of small choices and decisions that can transform your life.

....

....

Living a day without planning leaves you discouraged and fatigued.

....

....

....

....

One of life's most challenging decisions is determining whether to put in more effort or walk away.

♥ *Life's most profound lessons are often learned during the most challenging times and from our most significant mistakes.*

Everything happens for a reason. Live it. Love it. Learn from it.

> *One of the happiest moments ever is when you finally have the courage to let go of what you can't change.*

Whatever you do, do it with all your heart.

We close our eyes when we pray, dream, kiss, or cry because the most heart-touching moments in life can only be felt, not seen, by the heart.

Train your mind to see good in everything. Glass is half full and not half empty. Gratitude turns what we have into enough.

♥ *The way we choose to see the world creates the world we see. Life is a reflection of one's own consciousness.*

Just because you are struggling does not mean you are failing. Achieving any significant success involves facing and overcoming some form of struggle. Opportunity always comes with opposition. Hang in there.

Failure is part of success.

Life begins when you decide not to let another person or event control your emotions. Take a moment each day to ensure your emotional remote control is in your hands, with no one else pushing the buttons.

The universe only gives three answers to Prayer:

- Yes
- Not yet
- I have something better in mind

❤❤ You cannot go back and change the beginning, but you can start where you are and change the ending.

Stress is a psychological response to life's challenges. It is not about what happens to us but our response to those events. Our response is something that we can always control and change.

Don't just go through life; strive to grow through life.

❤ You have to die a few times before you can really live.

❤ Don't treat people as bad as they are, treat them as good as you are.

99

Whatever comes, let it come. What stays, let it stay. What goes, let it go.

♥ *Close some doors, not out of ego, limitation, pride, or arrogance, but simply because they no longer lead anywhere.*

♥ *Silence is better than nonsense.*

Notes to Self

*Never stop trying.
Never stop believing.
Never give up. Your
day will come.*

Mind is a beautiful servant of the heart and a
dangerous master of the ego.

Not everyone will comprehend your journey,
and that's alright. Your purpose is to live
your life, not to ensure everyone understands.

You are an angel in human form. You are
here to experience and learn life. Don't sink
in life, swim through life.

Sometimes you have to be your own hero.
Because the people you can't live without can
live without you.

__Beyond Begging: Love Without Compromise:__

Don't beg for love.

Don't beg someone to stay.

Don't beg someone to be with you.

Don't beg someone to come back or stay.

Don't beg for attention, commitment,

affection, loyalty, time or effort.

You should never have to ask to feel wanted.

If someone doesn't willingly give you these things with their arms wide open, they aren't worth it.

❤ ❤ ❤

What's yours is always yours. What's not yours was never really yours.

What's gone is good. What's coming is the best.

Love all. Trust few. Everything is real but not everyone is true.

> *True wisdom is knowing when to disengage from situations and individuals that pose a threat to your self-respect, inner peace, morals, values, and self-worth.*

Charity begins at home. Self-care, self-love is the first step to loving others.

When words are both true and kind, they can change the world.

You get what you work for not what you wish for.

I hold the key to my peace; nobody can hurt me without my permission.

The universal laws are divine tools to assist you in manifesting your version of paradise on earth.

You are not important to some people.
Move on.

....
....
....

Your present situation is not your final
destination. The best is yet to come.

....
....
....

One bad chapter does not mean your story is
over.

....
....
....

Your mind is the limit. You can attract
anything you want if you set your mind on it.

....
....
....

♥ The mind is everything. What you think,
you attract. Just for today, be positive.

....
....
....
....
....
....

If your compassion does not include self-compassion, it is incomplete.

Everything that has a beginning has an end. Everything is changing. Find peace in accepting this, and all will be well.

Guard your heart and mind wisely; Avoid becoming overly attached to someone unless they reciprocate, as one-sided expectations can have a detrimental impact on your mental well-being.

Peace comes from within. Do not seek it without. True tranquility resides in the depths of your own being.

Happy people build their inner world. Unhappy people blame their outer world.

P.A.I.N.S.

Positive attitude In negative situations.

Impossible says I'm possible.

> Having somewhere to go
> is HOME. Having
> someone to love is
> FAMILY. Having both is a
> BLESSING.

When you wish good for others, good things
come back to you. This is one of the laws of
nature.

Zeal will bring success.

Don't believe in fear and limitations.
Believe in yourself and in faith, embrace the
uncertainty of life, welcome the day with
a positive mindset, and let the day unfold,
knowing that only the best will happen.

Fear is of the unknown. Faith is in the
unknown. Both fear and faith pertain to
something that is yet to happen in the future.
It's up to you what you want to attract.
You attract what you believe. What are you
manifesting for your future?

If you are breathing you have a purpose. You are part of the divine plan.

Life is in the water, not fish. God is life. Let the divine flow through you. Stay unattached to the events unfolding in your life, for they are all part of the divine plan.

♥ *If you dialed up your self-belief to the max, what blockbuster life would you script, and how brilliantly would the story of your life unfold?*

♥♥ *Unleash the magic: Self-belief is your passport to manifesting the life you've always dreamed of. Take the first step by believing in yourself.*

If you don't have a vision, you will always fall back on the past.

Fear is not real; it is an illusory phantom of the ego, a false self of the egoic mind. Fear dims the brilliance of your true, authentic self. Don't let anyone or anything dim your light.

Choose to be a witness to your thoughts, emotions, and feelings. Avoid acting on them impulsively.

Your own mind can either be your greatest enemy or your strongest ally. It has the power to uplift you or put you down. There is no other enemy outside of you. You have the ability to control your mind and turn it into your best friend. A mind that loses control can become your enemy.

- *Not everybody is going to like you. Not everybody is going to accept you.*
- *You can't reach your destiny without some people being against you.*
- *If it's not between you and your destiny, it is a distraction.*

Chase your dreams and run your race anyway...

Unpleasant emotions, feelings, and
experiences are not real. Don't be fooled by
the storm; they are just passing clouds in the
vast sky of your true reality. Remember,
you've weathered many storms in the past,
and like those, this too shall pass.

You are bigger than your distractions.

Judging others, judging oneself, passing
opinions on people and situations, and
gossiping—all lower your vibration.

My life story is mine to write. I will not allow
others to dictate it, nor will I apologize for the
edits I make.

Angels honor your free will. They can move mountains for you. They don't get to action unless you invite them to do so. So just for today, pray.

Don't be in such a rush to figure out everything. Embrace the uncertainty and let your life surprise you.

Rome was not built in a day.

Don't seek happiness in others; it can leave you feeling alone. Find it within yourself, and you'll experience joy even in solitude. Happiness is a virtue.

Each morning we are born again. What we do today is what matters most.

Health is the ultimate gift, contentment the richest wealth, and faithfulness the magic ingredient for the best relationships.

The mind is like water. When it's turbulent, it's difficult to see. When it's calm, everything becomes clear.

Happiness is a choice, not an outcome.

> 66
> - *What you think, you become.*
> - *What you feel, you attract.*
> - *What you imagine, you create.*
> 99

Life is a wheel of happiness, sadness, tough times, and good times. If you're navigating through tough times, have faith that good times are on the way.

The best time for new beginnings is now.

Love the life you live. Live the life you love.

A teacher appears when the student is ready—a timeless wisdom echoing that the universe presents opportunities when you are ready to receive.

Life is the most challenging exam. Many people stumble because they attempt to imitate others, failing to recognize that each person has a unique question paper.

The heart is like a garden. It can foster fear or nurture compassion, cultivate resentment or bloom with love. What seeds will you choose to plant there?

Embracing the notion that 'you are not the doer' unveils a profound truth — we are but puppets in the greater universal dance, mere instruments in the hands of the creator. Don't resist the divine plan of life. Remember life is in the water, not the fish.

If you maintain an optimistic outlook in a negative situation, you are a winner.

Life has two rules:

* *Never quit*

* *Always remember rule #1.*

Keys to Peaceful Living:

- *Don't judge others.*

- *Don't worry about what others say.*

- *Enjoy each and every day.*

- *Give to the less fortunate.*

- *Make peace with your past.*

- *Be kind.*

- *You make your own happiness.*

I am not a product of circumstances. I am a product of my decisions.

♥ Let your smile change the world. But don't let the world change your smile.

Never lose sight of your blessings. There's plenty to be grateful for, so why focus on the negative?

You have to raise your vibration to connect with your angels. They can lower theirs only to a certain level. Align your frequency to hear their guidance.

Words twisted, it's a lie; words played, it's a joke. Words relied upon, it's ignorance. Transcend words, and become wise.

If you truly understood the power of positive thoughts, you would never allow a negative thought to linger in your mind. The key to transforming your life lies in cultivating a positive mindset.

....

....

Life is a journey to be experienced. Not a problem to be solved.

....

....

Once upon a time, you were a little kid with big dreams that you promised you'd make real one day. Don't disappoint yourself.

....

....

....

....

....

....

....

....

....

Millionaires are made in recession. Transform your challenges into opportunities for prosperity. Just one thought can turn your life upside down.

♥ No matter how you feel, get up, dress up, show up, and never give up.

Cleanliness is next to Godliness.

The secret to living is giving.

I am gonna make the rest of my life, the best of my life.

No expectations. No disappointments.

I don't have time to hate you because I am too busy loving my loved ones.

If you don't control your mind, someone else will.

The most challenging journey is the one you take alone, yet it is that very journey that builds your strength and takes you to the next version of yourself.

....

....

Nothing can hurt you as much as your own unguarded thoughts.

....

....

At times, you may not realize the weight of something you've been carrying for so long until you experience the relief of its release.

....

....

In times of turmoil, those who unwaveringly stand by you are your true family. The true family extends beyond blood.

....

....

....

....

....

....

♥ Decide what kind of life you really want.... and then, say NO to everything that isn't that.

The only true religion is having a compassionate heart.

Never be sad for someone who lets you down; simply smile and say, Thank you for the opportunity to discover someone better than you.

I forgive others who poured their pain onto me. I forgive myself for holding that pain for so long. I now release all negative energy that no longer serves me.

My words heal, bless, prosper, and strengthen me and others.

99

<u>Give</u>, without
getting misused.
<u>Love</u>, without
getting abused.
<u>Trust</u>, without
getting duped.
<u>Listen</u>, without
losing your voice.

99

The world doesn't need more successful people. It desperately craves more peacemakers, healers, restorers, storytellers, and lovers of all kinds.

Be the change you want to see in the world.

♥ I refuse to play the victim. I want my struggle, my pain, and my battle of life to make me someone's hero.

Recognizing when to walk away is wisdom. Having the strength to do so is courage. Walking away with your head held high is dignity.

Learn from everyone. Follow no one but your heart.

You see a person's true colors when you are no longer beneficial to their life.

♥ *If someone treats you poorly, remember that something is wrong with them, not you. Normal people don't go around destroying others.*

Remember your three R's:

• *Respect yourself*

• *Respect others*

• *Responsible for your actions*

Your best teacher is your last mistake.

If you don't go after what you want, you'll never have it. If you don't ask, the answer is no. If you don't step forward, you're always in the same place.

The greatest loss in life is not death; it's what dies within us while we are still alive.

Five things to level up your life:

* Quit people-pleasing

* Don't fear change

* Live in the present

* Invest in self-worth and self-belief

* Stop overthinking

Refrain from responding when you're angry, abstain from making promises when you're elated, and avoid making decisions when you're sad.

I hurt at places you couldn't imagine, at a level beyond comprehension. If you could feel this pain for just a day you'd see how strong I am.

Love is ....

uncomplicated

Communicate with your children as if they are the most knowledgeable, compassionate, and lovely individuals on the planet, for what they believe is what they will grow to be.

Do not rely on anyone. Even your shadow abandons you in the darkness.

Life is only as good as your mindset.

Everything – including love, hate, and suffering needs food to continue. If suffering continues, it's because we keep feeding our suffering.

Never confuse what you are offered, with what you're worth.

God assigns His most challenging battles to His most resilient soldiers. Through the darkest night, the brightest stars reveal themselves. God knows your strength. The battles are for you to realize you are stronger than you know.

In the story of life, there are sad, happy, tough, and exciting chapters. Life never stops surprising you. Turning the page is the only way to reveal the wonders of the next chapter.

Failure is success in progress.

Consistency is the key.

The strongest hearts have the most scars.

Don't say "Why me". I say "Try me".

When life hits you hard to the ground. Get up, brush off, and say "You hit me like a B****".

....
....

If you feel like you've endured enough, then it's time for you to let go and move on to better things.

....
....

The depth of pain isn't always reflected in tears; it's sometimes hidden behind the smile we wear.

....
....

♥ Keep going. Everything you need will come to you at the perfect time.

....
....

♥♥ Don't be jealous of a person who is always smiling because they know the value of every moment. They have seen the worst of life. Next time you see a smiling person, hug them because they are spreading positivity despite hardships.

♥ The best thing you can ever do is to believe in yourself.

Do not permit someone to mistreat you simply because you love them.

Don't let yourself be controlled by three things: money, people, and past experiences.

Just like electric currents, the right relationships can light up your life, while wrong connections can short-circuit it.

You cannot heal in the same environment where you got sick.

Serenity is found when you replace expectations with acceptance.

Never forget the people who take time out of their day to check up on you.

Be happy not because everything is good, but because you see good in everything.

Pay attention; the way someone treats you speaks volumes.

You define your own life. Don't let people write your script.

Change is never painful. Only the resistance to change is painful.

Live without pretending. Love without depending. Listen without defending. Speak without offending.

Life is a profound teacher; it repeats lessons until they're learned.

No matter how poorly someone treats you, never stoop to their level. Stay composed, stand strong, and choose to walk away.

Don't change so people will like you. Be yourself and the right people will love the real you.

Nothing ever goes away until it has taught us what we need to know.

You are the victor, not the victim.

Forgiveness is next to Godliness.

Practice the Pause:

* *Pause before judging*

* *Pause before assuming*

* *Pause before accusing*

* *Pause before doubting*

* *Pause before reacting*

* *Pause before doing something impulsive*

* *Pause before saying something regretful*

❤ ❤ ❤

Life is beautiful. Each day, each hour and each minute will not come again in your entire life. So avoid fights, and anger and speak kindly to every person.

God is steering an airplane while you are driving a car. God changes the direction of your journey because God sees things you don't. Keep moving forward with faith.

Always be thankful for what you have, many people have nothing.

Give, even if you have only a little.

♥ Someone who does not understand your silence will probably not understand your words.

Exercising patience in moments of anger can spare you from many days of sorrow.

Your problem isn't the problem, it's your reaction that is the problem.

Without communication, there is no
relationship. Without respect, there is no love.
Without trust, there's no reason to continue.

One day you will be blessed with everything
you ever asked for. Have faith even in the
dark days.

I wake up with a peaceful mind and a
grateful heart.

Do it now; sometimes 'later' becomes 'never'.

Remember that once you dreamed of being
where you are now.

We don't have to be smarter than others, just
more disciplined than our past selves.

To be kind is more important than to be right. Sometimes, what people need is not a brilliant mind that speaks but a special heart that listens.

Anger is a self-inflicted punishment for the mistakes of others.

The less you care about what people think, the happier you will be.

♥ My scars tell a silent story, proof that life's attempts to break me were in vain.

No anger inside means no enemy outside.

If you want to fly, give up everything that weighs you down.

- If you are depressed, you are living in the past.
- If you are anxious, you are living in the future.
- If you are at peace, you are living in the present.

If people don't make an effort to be in your life don't try so hard to be in theirs. It's not worth it.

Happiness is not a destination it is a way of life.

No great thing can be achieved from the comfort zone.

❤ *If you are still looking for that one person who will change your life, take a look in the mirror.*

If the plan does not work change the plan, not the goal.

❤❤ *A good relationship is when someone accepts your past, supports your present, loves and encourages your future.*

♥ *Practice like you've never won. Perform like you've never lost.*

You owe yourself a big apology for putting up with what you didn't deserve.

God puts people in your life for a reason and removes them from your life for a <u>better</u> reason.

I apologize, but I've moved beyond the days of chasing people. If you're not making the effort to be in my life, don't be surprised if I choose to ignore you for the rest of my life.

Your confidence stems from living as your true, authentic self. No opinion, rejection, or behavior can shake you when you embrace your true self.

Stop worrying about people that aren't worrying about you.

Don't overthink how to get everything done. Begin, learn along the way, and everything will fall into place. Taking action generates momentum, and momentum fuels your motivation to persevere.

A challenge is akin to the tail of an animal - before it is presented to you, God has already crafted the solution. Every challenge in life is inherently solvable.

Sometimes not getting what you want is a stroke of good luck.

Stop allowing individuals who contribute so little to your life to have such a significant influence over your thoughts, feelings, and emotions. Remember, they are living in your mind rent-free.

Food for thought

- $1^{365} = 1$

- $1.01^{365} = 37.78$

Devoting just 0.01% of each day to self-care can lead to a transformation of 37.78%, compared to your previous self.

A single positive thought in the morning can set the tone for your entire day.

Always remember, the sun, the moon, and the truth cannot be long hidden.

A vision can be as simple as being yourself and showing up as your best self each day. The universe is waiting to reward joyful people.

Every day is like Groundhog Day. Take a moment to reflect on your previous day and consider how you can improve today to become the best version of yourself. Soon, you'll notice that you're creating the life you want. Don't forget to include forgiveness and compassion in your considerations.

Every day, we are born again. What you do today is what matters most.

> *You either suffer the pain of discipline or suffer the pain of regret.*

♥ If life can take away someone you never imagined losing, it has the potential to introduce someone you never dreamed of having.

Slow down. Calm down. Don't worry. Don't hurry. Trust the process.

Don't compare your life to others. There's no comparison between the sun and the moon. They shine when it's their time.

A healthy relationship is built on two key elements: appreciating the commonalities and honoring the differences.

I don't hate you. I just lost respect for you.

A few tears won't kill you, only heal you. A little pain won't destroy you, only strengthen you. So cry, forgive, and move on.

God has a plan. Trust it. Live it. Enjoy it.

If someone desires to be in your life, they will earnestly make an effort to be part of it. No explanations. No justifications.

Be with someone who brings out the best in you, not the stress in you.

Without self-discipline, success is impossible, period.

Stay away from negative people. They have a problem for every solution.

Forgiving you is my gift to you. Moving on is my gift to myself.

There are two types of pain: one that hurts you and the other that propels you to level up.

Every next level of your life will demand a different version of you.

When you let go, you create space for better things to enter your life.

Prayer is talking to the universe. Meditation is listening to the universe.

♥ Experiencing what you don't want can sometimes lead to a deeper understanding of what you really want.

Let go of the pain, but hold on to the lessons gained.

When you care about what others think, you will always be their slave.

To heal a wound you should stop touching it.

Someone who conquers themselves through self-control and discipline is genuinely invincible and unstoppable.

If you do not experience anything, it's impossible to gain knowledge.

If you don't want anyone to find out, don't do it.

Don't fear slow progress; fear not moving forward at all.

If you know yourself, you will not be harmed by what is said about you.

Don't let what you cannot do interfere with what you can do.

If you can't help others, at least don't hurt them.

If you survived a storm you won't be bothered by the rain.

Maturity starts when drama ends.

♥ *True peace comes from knowing that the Universe (the creator) is in control.*

Dear Heart

Resist the urge to involve yourself in everything you feel!

xoxo

♥♥ I am the creator of my feelings, thoughts and words. No one else.

The smile on my face doesn't imply my life is perfect. It signifies my gratitude for what I have and what I am blessed with.

One of the most heart-wrenching aspects of a relationship is when your feelings are one-sided.

I am better for all the things that have happened to me, the good and the bad.

You are not a rehabilitation center for poorly raised partners. Your role isn't to fix, change, or parent them. Seek a partner, not a project.

If a person is sensitive, they won't do unto others what they wouldn't want done unto them.

Relax and you will find that everything is falling in the right place.

Both convenience and commitment bring comfort to the body, mind, and soul. The key is to strike a balance between the two.

Every single day ask yourself after doing a task, "Was this my best? Work on it until your answer is "Yes".

__Benjamin Franklin's Thirteen Virtues:__

* *Temperance*

* *Silence*

* *Order*

* *Resolution*

* *Frugality*

* *Industry*

* *Sincerity*

* *Justice*

* *Moderation*

* *Cleanliness*

* *Tranquility*

* *Chastity*

* *Humility*

♥ Prayer isn't about asking God for things; it's more like trusting that God knows what's good for you and believing that only the best will happen. Having this confidence in yourself is prayer. Confidence in yourself and in God is essentially synonymous.

Serenity Prayer

Dear Lord,

Grant me the calmness to accept the unchangeable, the courage to transform what I can, and the wisdom to discern the difference. Amen.

Procrastination Prayer

Dear Lord,

Keep me attached to the desk until the work is done. Amen.

<u>Just For Today Prayer</u>

♥ *Just for today,*

• *I choose not to worry.*

• *I choose not to harbor anger.*

• *I opt for kindness to every living being.*

• *I express gratitude for all my blessings.*

• *I handle my duties and responsibilities with integrity.*

• *I embody compassion and forgiveness.*

• *I discover joy in life's smallest gifts.*

• *I experience a sense of peace.*

• *I do everything with passion.*

• *I believe in myself more.*

• *I dare to dream big.*

♥♥♥

The universe is saying to you today:

Once you decide to have a good life, the universe will orchestrate its alignment for you to have that good life. The people you need will appear. The healing you need will happen. The doors you need will unlock. Once you truly and sincerely decide, miracles will happen.

Journey through the dark night of the soul...

Along the shore, 'neath the moon's soft glow,

I tread a path, laden with woe.

In the sands of time, my journey unfolds,

A lone sojourn where stories are told.

Imprints mark the steps I take,

A solitary voyage, forlorn heartache.

Yet, in the struggles that weigh me down,

One set of footprints, a mystery profound.

"Lord," I questioned, my voice a plea,

"Why, in my trials, do I not see,

Your presence near when shadows loom,

Why face the darkness in solitude's gloom?"

The answer came in whispers, gentle and wise,

"My child, in your pain, hear this surprise.

In the lone prints, when despair holds tight,

I carried you through the darkest night."

Through life's storms, when tempests brew,

In footprints etched where dreams once grew,

A story of solace, a presence so clear,

Guiding my steps, dispelling all fear.

In the sands of time, a tale engraved,

Footprints of grace, where love is paved.

A testament, where shadows depart,

The footprints of a compassionate heart.

Commentary:

A poem inspired by 'Footprints in the Sand,' this piece portrays a journey of solitude, struggle, divine guidance, and the legacy of a compassionate and grace-filled life. By walking in the footsteps of compassion and holding onto faith in the divine, one can journey through life's shadows, guided by the grace of the divine.

❤ ❤ ❤

Life "Commandments":

- Love God more than anything else.

- Don't make anything in your life more important than God.

- Always utter God's name with love and reverence.

- Respect God by taking a day of rest every seventh day of the week.

- Love and respect your mom and dad.

- Never hurt anyone.

- Always be faithful to your spouse.

- Don't take anything that isn't yours.

- Always tell the truth.

- Be happy with what you have. Don't wish for other people's things.

❤ ❤ ❤

Millionaire Mindset:

It's not about how you start; it's about how you finish... The secret to the success of millionaires does not lie in:

- Rising early

- Having a perfect morning routine

- Practicing mindfulness and exercise

- Cultivating gratitude and compassion

- Maintaining a healthy diet

- Utilizing productivity hacks and apps

The answer lies in mental mastery—the ability to control your thoughts and act in spite of fear. All of the above are essential tools to unlock the door to mastery and pave your way to success!

❤ ❤ ❤

<u>Beyond my influence:</u>

* *My history*

* *What lies ahead*

* *Others' conduct*

* *Others' viewpoints*

* *Events in my surroundings*

* *Others' perceptions of me*

* *The results of my endeavors*

* *How others tend to themselves*

Within my sphere of influence:

* *My limits*

* *My thoughts and deeds*

* *My objectives*

* *Where I direct my energy*

* *The way I talk to myself*

* *How I navigate challenges*

❤ ❤ ❤

I am not responsible for:

- *Maintaining anyone's happiness*

- *My trauma (but I am responsible for my healing)*

- *Their reactions to my boundaries*

- *Their perception of me*

- *Someone else's growth*

- *Affairs beyond my control*

- *Others' insecurities*

- *Choices and actions of my loved ones*

♥ ♥ ♥

A Letter from Your Future Self

Dear Self ♥,

Nine pieces of advice to become a better version of yourself.

- *You are in the exact place that you're meant to be; nothing is off schedule, nothing is remotely wrong—everything is right on track. Forgive the past, look forward, have a vision, and move forward.*

- *If prayers get answered, there is a reason. If prayers do not get answered, there is a better reason. Embrace the uncertainty and have faith that only the best will happen to you.*

- *Feelings are like visitors. Don't base your decisions on fleeting emotions.*

- *Don't be sad or hurt. Your sadness comes from resisting a change that God is orchestrating to propel you toward your destiny.*

- With 8 billion people on the planet, there could be 8 billion businesses, and each person can have 8 billion followers, including you. The universe is that abundant. Strive to be on a creative plane, not a competitive one.

- You are unique. You are you. The sun and moon shine in their own time.

- Deny all negative information from your consciousness.

- Be the blessing the world needs today—in everything you do and in everything you say. This world needs more love, kindness, peace, and harmony.

- Dream big. Believe in yourself more. Believe in the beauty of your dreams.

Love you Always

It's me,

Your Future Self ♥

ABOUT THE AUTHOR

Sneha Bandaru, an engineer with over 20 years of experience in the semiconductor industry, has made significant contributions to the development of SoC chips for various devices, including laptops, servers, and smartphones. In her leisure time, she enjoys reading self-development books. She is an ardent follower and lifelong student of Sri Sri Ravi Shankar, who envisions a stress-free and violence-free world. Sneha Bandaru expresses deep gratitude for the valuable influence that her success coach, Mo Faul, has had in her life, guiding her toward becoming the best version of herself.

ABOUT THE BOOK

The last thought or feeling you sleep with at night is the thought or feeling you wake up with, and that feeling defines your state of mind and sets the tone for the entire day. Challenge yourself to keep both the first and last thoughts positive. Flipping through a few pages of this diary to uplift your mood is a great way to unwind the mind chatter and rewire the mind for positive thinking. It has rekindled my spirit in rough times, and I hope it does the same for you.

In my moments of darkness, I've sought knowledge to uplift me. Over the years, my journal became a sanctuary filled with uplifting insights. Motivated by a desire to offer my 12-year-old son (as of 2023) guidance through life's challenges, I decided to share this source of inspiration with a broader audience. This book is not just for my son but for teens, young adults, and anyone seeking inspiration. We all need a push from time to time, and this diary is my way of extending that support to the world.

This diary is a source of inspiration to brighten your mood during rough days. It has an assorted collection of life quotes, paraphrases, motivational sayings, encouraging phrases, words of wisdom, uplifting maxims, inspiring mantras, and a thought-provoking future-self letter.

From the bottom of my heart, with gratitude ♥.